The Gourmet
Peanut Butter
Cookbook

© annabelle pisani

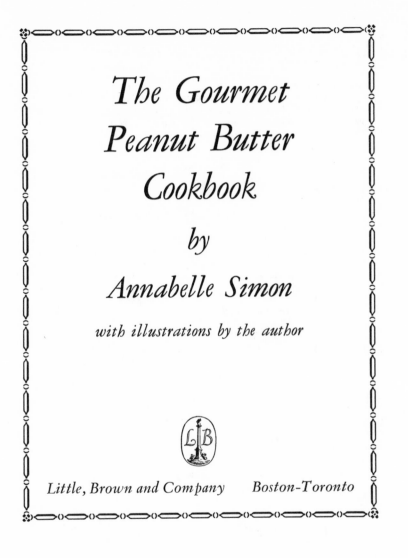

The Gourmet
Peanut Butter
Cookbook

by

Annabelle Simon

with illustrations by the author

Little, Brown and Company   Boston-Toronto

FIRST EDITION

T 05/75

Library of Congress Cataloging in Publication Data

Simon, Annabelle.
    The gourmet peanut butter cookbook.

    Includes index.
    1. Cookery (Peanuts)   2. Peanut butter.   I.   Title.
TX803.P35S55   641.6′3   74-28122
ISBN 0-316-79150-4 pbk.

Designed by D. Christine Benders

Published simultaneously in Canada
by Little, Brown & Company (Canada) Limited

PRINTED IN THE UNITED STATES OF AMERICA

To Katherine and Joanne who laughed with me,
and especially to Walter, who hates peanut butter

INTRODUCTION

꙰)━◦━◦━◦━◦━◦━◦━◦━◦━◦━◦━◦━(꙰

Almost every American child has had some memorable experience with peanut butter. It was a staple item in my diet until the day I came home from school with a twenty-four-hour virus which I attributed to a peanut butter and jelly sandwich. I was certain I could never endure the sight of those ingredients again.

Only recently have I rediscovered the qualities of the goober and largely by accident.

While living abroad, I developed a craving for certain remembered but unavailable foods, among them, to my surprise, peanut butter. I would enter any venerable French delicatessen filled with beautifully prepared and decorated foods and ask for a jar of peanut butter, to the vendor's disgust and my chagrin when he could not supply it. I have since discovered that my experience has been shared by many who have spent long periods out of the country.

In the course of satisfying my craving, I have found that the effect of peanut butter on the palate can be transformed when it is combined with other, unlikely, ingredients. Given the importance of peanut butter as a high source of protein, this trait should be further explored.

Contrary to popular belief, the peanut (goober, groundnut, monkey nut, pinder, earthnut, Manila nut) is not a nut, but a pea derived from a tender, annual vine of the legume family *(Arachis hypogaea)*. It flowers aboveground, then the withered stalk forces the ovary underground, where it matures. There are many types of peanuts, including runners (eight varieties), Spanish (ten varieties), Valencia, Virginia (nineteen varieties) and Tennessee Red.

The peanut is cheaply and easily grown, and easy to harvest. Though not particular about what it grows in, it favors light sandy soil with plenty of lime. It was first found in Brazil or Peru and introduced into Africa by missionaries. Traders brought it to North America, supplying it as food for slaves on ship crossings. Nowadays it is a staple food in Malaysia, parts of Africa, and the United States. While grown in over forty countries, the leading producers are India, mainland China, Nigeria, Senegal, and the United States. The principal producers in this country are Alabama, Georgia, North Carolina, Oklahoma, Texas, and Virginia.

The growth in production and range of experimentation in the past fifty years has been remarkable, due largely to the inventions, around 1900, of equipment for planting, cultivating, harvesting, picking, shelling, and roasting peanuts. Further impetus was given by the crop failures of 1920, when farmers in Georgia, Alabama, and Florida were forced to find substitutes for cotton ravaged by the boll weevil. By the Second World War, peanuts had become a strategic crop grown for food.

It was in the nineteen twenties and thirties that George Washington

Carver stimulated an interest in the potential of the peanut through his researches. Since his death, studies and investigations have continued, with significant results.

Though it is largely the seeds of the peanut plant that concern us in this book, the hulls have also been put to good use as fuel in industries processing the nuts. Small quantities are used as a fertilizer diluent and as stable bedding and fodder for livestock. Research has indicated that peanut hulls can be used as a stubstitute for cork in the manufacture of linoleum, as a filler in plastics and dynamite, as an aid in refining lubricating oils, and as an active carbon used to deodorize, decolorize, or clarify such products as raw sugar.

The great nutritive value of the nut itself has long been recognized. A pound of peanuts has more protein than a pound of steak and provides twice as much food energy. It yields an oil of superior quality. The clean cake, after the oil has been removed, is very high in protein and produces a meal especially prized by bakers and confectioners. In addition, a peanut cheese has been produced which may some day rival cheeses made from milk.

The history of peanut butter is somewhat obscure. It was first made commercially by a St. Louis physician around 1890, who recommended it to his patients because of its high protein and low carbohydrate content. By the turn of the century, many people were grinding their own at home. Despite its ever-presence in sandwiches, cookies, and candies, it is used less as an ingredient in main dishes than it should be.

This book provides a representative offering of the more interesting recipes and does not attempt to be encyclopedic. In the interest of good eating and good fun, read on!

CONTENTS

❖❯❮❯❮❯❮❯❮❯❮❯❮❯❮❯❮❯❮❯❮❯❮❖

The Gourmet
Peanut Butter
Cookbook

How to Make Your Own Peanut Butter

Large cans of shelled peanuts can be purchased in supermarkets. Either hulled or unhulled nuts may be used. The unhulled add flavor and texture to the blend.

Place 1 cup of peanuts in a blender. Depending upon the markings on your particular machine, you may have to break up the peanuts in a mortar and pestle beforehand. Add 1 or 2 tablespoons of oil, preferably peanut oil, to assist blending. Run the machine until you achieve the smoothness you like. You may add some or all of the following if you wish: a pinch of salt, 1 teaspoon honey or sugar, 1 tablespoon wheat germ.

If you do not want to make your own, the unhydrogenated peanut butter sold in health-food stores is almost as good.

You can also substitute commercial peanut butter in all the recipes in this book, but the consistency is not the same and the commercial variety will not always respond as well.

DIPS AND APPETIZERS

Annabelle's Peanut Butter Dip

2 tablespoons peanut butter
6 slices white bread
2 tablespoons vinegar
½ lemon

2-3 cloves garlic
2 tablespoons yoghurt or
    sour cream
Salt and pepper to taste

Soak the bread in water, then squeeze out the excess. Blend all the ingredients together in a blender. Let the mixture stand for 12 hours. Serve with toasted Arabic bread or a mild cracker.

The recipe is sufficient for a large party and is mercifully inexpensive.

Goober Dip

1-3 cloves garlic
Juice of 3 lemons

2-3 tablespoons peanut butter
2 tablespoons chopped parsley

½ teaspoon ground cumin
  (see glossary)
1 small can anchovy fillets,
  drained and chopped, or 2
  pickled herrings and a medium-

sized Spanish onion, sliced

GARNISH

1 hard-boiled egg, sliced
Additional chopped parsley

Blend the garlic, lemon juice, peanut butter, 2 tablespoons parsley and the cumin together. To the blended mixture add either the anchovy fillets or the herrings and onion. Garnish with the additional parsley and the sliced hard-boiled egg.

Serve with toasted bread for dipping. Makes about 1 cup

Garbanzo Dip

AMERICAN HUMMUS

1½ cups fresh chick-peas, soaked
  overnight, or 1 can (20
  ounces) Mexican chick-peas
Juice of 2-3 lemons, or to taste
2-3 cloves garlic
Salt
2-3 tablespoons peanut butter
1 pinch of cayenne pepper
  (optional)

GARNISH

A few whole chick-peas (see
  below)
1 tablespoon olive oil
1 teaspoon paprika
1 tablespoon finely chopped
  parsley

Boil the soaked chick-peas in fresh water for about 1 hour, or until they are soft; the cooking time will depend on their age and quality (omit this step if you are using the canned ones). Drain them and put aside a few whole ones to use as a garnish. Press the rest through a sieve or use an electric mixer or blender to reduce them to a puree. If the latter, pour the lemon juice and a little water into the bowl or container first, to provide enough liquid for successful blending. Add the remaining ingredients and blend to a creamy paste, adding more water if necessary.

If you are blending by hand, crush the garlic cloves with the salt, add them to the crushed chick-peas, and pound them all together until they are well mixed. Add the peanut butter gradually, followed by the lemon juice. If the mixture is too thick, thin it with water and lemon juice to the consistency of a creamy mayonnaise. Keep tasting and adjusting the seasoning, adding more lemon juice, garlic salt, and cayenne as necessary.

Pour the dip into a serving dish, combine the olive oil and paprika, and dribble the mixture over the surface. Sprinkle with the chopped parsley and arrange a decorative pattern of whole chick-peas on top.

Serve with toasted Arabic bread for dipping. Makes about 2 cups.

This dip goes well with bread, fish, eggplant — practically anything — and can also be used as an appetizer. Serves 4 to 6

Peanut Butter–Yoghurt Dip

2-3 cloves garlic
Salt

2-3 tablespoons peanut butter
½ cup yoghurt

Juice of 2½ lemons, or more   GARNISH
   as needed   *Finely chopped parsley*

Crush the garlic with a little salt and mix it with the peanut butter. Add the yoghurt and lemon juice gradually, beating vigorously to make a smooth, thick cream. Taste and add more salt, lemon juice, or garlic if necessary. In an electric blender everything can be added at once.

Pour the mixture into a bowl, garnish with the parsley, and provide toasted bread for dipping. The dip can also be served as an accompaniment to broiled meat and salads. Makes about 1 cup

Eggplant Dip

AMERICAN BABA GHANOUSH

The harmony of flavors depends largely on the size and flavor of the eggplants, with the other ingredients added to taste. The quantities specified give a fairly large amount, enough for a dip at a party.

3 large eggplants   *2 tablespoons finely chopped*
2-4 cloves garlic   *parsley*
Salt   GARNISH
3 tablespoons peanut butter   *A few black olives or 1 tomato,*
Juice of 3 lemons   *thinly sliced*
½ teaspoon ground cumin
   (optional)

Bake or broil the eggplants until the skins blacken or blister, then peel and mash them, squeezing out as much of the bitter juice as possible. Crush the garlic cloves together with the salt, add to the mashed eggplant, and mix thoroughly. Next, add the peanut butter and lemon juice alternately, blending for a few seconds after each addition. Add more salt, lemon juice, garlic or peanut butter to taste. Add the cumin if desired.

Serve hot or cold, garnished with the black olives or tomato slices. Mild crackers should accompany it. It can also be served as an appetizer. Makes 3 to 4 cups

Variation: add 10 peeled, chopped cherry tomatoes to the mixture.

Curried Peanut Butter Dip with Chappatis

½ cup peanut butter
½ cup sour cream thinned with
  2 tablespoons milk, or ½ cup
  buttermilk
1 teaspoon curry powder (see
  glossary)

1 teaspoon Worcestershire sauce
Cayenne pepper to taste
¼ teaspoon salt
1 teaspoon chutney (optional)

Blend together the peanut butter and the sour cream or buttermilk. Stir in the rest of the ingredients. Serve with celery and carrot sticks or with some form of Indian bread, such as papadam, chapattis, or poorie. Makes 1 generous cup

CHAPATTIS

1 cup water

2 cups whole-meal flour

Pinch of salt

Add the water to the flour and salt to make a stiff dough. Knead well. Pinch off pieces of dough and roll them into balls the size of a walnut. Roll each ball in flour and roll out on a lightly floured breadboard or table to the thickness of a pancake. Heat a large frying pan without grease. Place the chapattis in the pan and fry for 2 minutes on each side. Add a little melted butter and continue to fry until golden brown. Eat while hot. Makes 18 to 24 chapattis

Fresh Pineapple Squares with Pork and Peanut Butter Topping

2 tablespoons vegetable oil

1 teaspoon finely chopped garlic

1 tablespoon finely chopped onion

1 teaspoon lean ground pork

¼ cup peanut butter

1 tablespoon sugar

½ teaspoon finely chopped fresh coriander root

1 teaspoon salt

¼ teaspoon white pepper

2 teaspoons cornstarch combined with 2 teaspoons cold water

1 small fresh pineapple

1 fresh hot red chili pepper sliced in slivers (see glossary)

Heat the oil in an 8- or 10-inch skillet, add the garlic and onion, and cook for 3 to 5 minutes, until soft and golden. Add the pork and cook until all the pink is gone. Add the peanut butter, sugar, coriander, salt, and white pepper; then add the cornstarch-and-water mixture. Simmer for 10 minutes over low heat, stirring constantly. Transfer the mixture to a bowl and cool to room temperature.

Peel the pineapple, slice into ½-inch rounds, remove the core, and cut the rounds into 1-inch pieces. Place the pieces on a serving dish and top each one with 1 teaspoon of the pork mixture and a chili sliver. Makes 12 to 18 squares

Chinese Fried Dumplings with Peanut Butter Sauce

FILLING

1 pound mushrooms

3½ cups finely chopped Chinese cabbage

3 cups ground pork

3½ tablespoons cornstarch

¼ teaspoon salt

1 egg white

1 tablespoon sherry

2 tablespoons soy sauce

½ teaspoon sugar

3 medium onions, chopped

1 tablespoon soy oil

DOUGH

3 cups sifted flour

1 tablespoon vegetable oil

1 cup boiling water

Extra vegetable oil for frying

SAUCE

6 teaspoons peanut butter

3 tablespoons chopped green onion

3 tablespoons chopped parsley

3 tablespoons soy sauce or tamari (see glossary)

3 tablespoons dry red wine

4 teaspoons wine vinegar

1 clove garlic, finely chopped

½ teaspoon ground dried red chili pepper

½ teaspoon anchovy paste

Pour boiling water over the mushrooms to cover and let them stand overnight. Drain, reserving the liquid, and chop them fine. In a large bowl, combine them with the rest of the filling ingredients and mix thoroughly. Add as much of the reserved liquid as needed to make the mixture moist.

To make the dough, place the flour in a bowl and add the vegetable oil and the cup of boiling water a little at a time, mixing to make a firm, nonsticky dough. Turn out on a floured board and knead until smooth and elastic (approximately 15 minutes). Let stand 30 minutes under a damp cloth. Shape into a sausage 2 inches thick, cut in half, and roll each half to 1-inch thickness. Cut the halves into ¾-inch lengths (there should be at least 24 of them) and roll into thin ovals.

Fill the center of each oval with 1 tablespoon of filling. Fold over and pinch the edges. As you proceed, keep the finished dumplings on a lightly floured board and covered with a damp cloth.

Place the dumplings in a 12-inch skillet and add ¾ cup of boiling water, cover, and simmer 7 to 10 minutes. Remove the dumplings and discard any remaining liquid. Heat 2 tablespoons of vegetable oil in

the skillet, add a few dumplings, and fry until golden brown on both sides, adding more oil as necessary.

Last, make the sauce by stirring all the ingredients together.

Serve the dumplings with wine vinegar and the peanut butter sauce. Serves 8 (three dumplings apiece)

Chicken Rolls

DOUGH

2 cups all-purpose flour

⅓ cup shortening

½ teaspoon salt

1 egg

¼ cup ice water

Vegetable oil, preferably peanut oil, for deep-frying

FILLING

1 pound cooked chicken meat

2 slices boiled ham, ⅛" thick

½ ounce green ginger (see glossary)

Salt and pepper to taste

3 scallions

SAUCE

1 teaspoon cornstarch

1 teaspoon salt

1 teaspoon sugar

Pinch of cayenne pepper

1 teaspoon sherry

1 tablespoon soy sauce

2-3 tablespoons peanut butter

1 tablespoon vegetable oil, preferably peanut oil

Make the dough by combining the flour, shortening, and salt, and blending them with the tips of the fingers. Add the egg and ice water and mix thoroughly. Chill in the refrigerator for at least half an hour.

Cut the chicken, ham, and ginger into thin strips. Chop the scallions fine. Season the chicken with salt and pepper, and let it stand for 15 minutes.

Roll the dough into a thin rectangle and cut into 3-inch squares (there should be at least 24). Spoon in some chicken, ham, ginger, and scallions, about 1 tablespoon in all on each square. Roll up like a sausage and deep-fry for 3 to 5 minutes in hot oil. Drain and serve with the sauce.

To make the sauce, place the cornstarch in a saucepan and stir in the remaining ingredients. Cook over low heat for 2 minutes, stirring constantly. Pour over rolls. Serves 8 (three rolls apiece)

Vegetarian Chopped Chicken Liver

½ pound string beans or 1
  package frozen lima beans
2 tablespoons vegetable oil
1 large onion, coarsely chopped
2 tablespoons tomato sauce

2 tablespoons peanut butter
1 bay leaf
Pinch of powdered mustard
Pinch of chili powder
Salt and pepper to taste

Cook the beans, drain, and set aside. Place the vegetable oil in a large skillet and sauté the onion until soft and translucent. Add the rest of the ingredients and blend. Remove the mixture from the heat and let it cool.

Chop all the ingredients together until fine but not entirely creamy. Serve as a spread, appetizer, or sandwich ingredient. Makes about 1½ cups

SOUPS

Peanut Butter Soup

2 tablespoons butter
2 tablespoons flour
4 cups milk
½ cup grated onion
2 tablespoons grated sharp
   cheddar cheese
¼ teaspoon celery seed

¼ teaspoon black pepper
1 bay leaf, finely crumbled
⅓ cup peanut butter
   GARNISH
Whole macaroons (optional)
Bacon bits

Melt the butter and combine it with the flour. Add the milk, then the remaining ingredients. Bring to a boil and simmer 15 minutes. Add the macaroons if desired. Garnish with bacon bits. Serve hot or cold. Serves 6 to 8

Black Bean Soup

1 pound dried black beans   *1 teaspoon dry mustard*
8 cups water   *1 cup finely chopped onion*
¼ pound salt pork   *1 tablespoon lemon juice*
4 tablespoons peanut butter   *½ teaspoon cayenne pepper*
2 cloves garlic, finely chopped   *Salt and pepper to taste*
1 teaspoon oregano

In a large casserole, soak the beans in the water overnight. Add the salt pork and simmer for 2½ hours or until almost tender.

In a separate skillet, combine the peanut butter, garlic, oregano, and dry mustard, and cook over a moderate flame for 1 minute stirring constantly. Next, add the onions and continue to cook and stir until they are transparent. Add the lemon juice, cayenne, and 1 cup of the bean liquid, and simmer for 15 minutes. Add everything to the casserole with the beans and continue to simmer for an additional ½ hour, or until the beans are tender. Add the salt and pepper.

Puree the soup in an electric blender, 1 cup at a time, and serve. Serves 6 to 8

Beef Soup

*1½ pounds stewing beef in
    chunks
1 tablespoon oil
2 cups water
2 medium onions, sliced
Salt and black pepper to taste*

*¼ teaspoon allspice
¼ teaspoon white pepper
1 package (10 ounces) frozen
    okra
1½ cups peanut butter
Sweet red pepper flakes to taste*

In a deep cast-iron or enamel skillet or casserole, brown the beef in the oil. Add all the water minus 1 tablespoon, the onion, salt, black pepper, allspice, and white pepper. Bring to a boil, lower the heat, cover, and simmer until tender (about 1 hour).

Cook the okra, drain, mash, and add to the beef.

In another pan, combine the peanut butter with 1 tablespoon water (to loosen the peanut butter) and heat until oil begins to collect on top. Keep pouring the oil off until it stops appearing in large quantities. Then gradually add the peanut butter to the beef mixture. If the soup is too thick, add water as needed. Then add the pepper flakes and reheat. Serves 6

Chicken Soup

*1 broiler chicken, 3-3½ pounds,
  quartered*
3 quarts water
¼ teaspoon salt
4 medium onions, 1 chopped
*1-2 cloves garlic, crushed with a
  mortar and pestle*
*2 tablespoons peanut or other
  vegetable oil*

3-4 tablespoons peanut butter
*1 teaspoon curry powder (see
  glossary)*
*1 slice green ginger (optional)
  (see glossary)*
*½ teaspoon freshly ground
  coriander*
Juice of 1 lemon

Combine the chicken, water, salt, and three of the onions in a large pot and simmer until tender (25 to 40 minutes). Remove the chicken, drain, and set aside, reserving the stock.

In a separate skillet, fry the chopped onion and garlic in the oil until they are clear and tender. Work the peanut butter into the sauté, then add the curry powder, ginger, and coriander. Add the mixture to the chicken stock and simmer over low heat for half an hour. Finally add the lemon juice.

The soup can be served by itself or poured over the chicken, which has been cut up into strips and placed in a deep serving bowl. Serves 12

Tomato Soup

1 can (16 ounces) tomato juice
1 cup milk
1 cup peanut butter
½ teaspoon Worcestershire or
  tabasco sauce
½ teaspoon seasoned salt
⅛ teaspoon black pepper

⅛ teaspoon cayenne pepper
GARNISH
2 hard-boiled eggs, sliced
Several sprigs of parsley,
  chopped
2 tablespoons coarsely chopped
  peanuts

Put the juice, milk, and peanut butter in a bowl and beat with a rotary beater until blended. Add the seasonings and heat. Garnish with the eggs, parsley, and peanuts. Serves 6

Oxtail Soup

1 oxtail
10 cups water
2 teaspoons salt
1 tablespoon peanut butter
¼ cup soy sauce

1 tablespoon peanut oil
½ teaspoon ground pepper
2 tablespoons finely chopped
  onion
1 tablespoon chopped garlic

Have the oxtail cut into 8 to 10 pieces. Wash and place in a pot with the water and salt. Bring to a boil and simmer, removing scum from the surface, for 3 hours or until tender. Remove the oxtail from the broth and cut away the fat.

Combine the remaining ingredients in a mixing bowl; add the oxtail and stir until it is well coated. Return everything to the broth and bring to a boil before serving. Serves 8 to 10

MEATS

Chili

2-3 tablespoons peanut oil
1 pound ground beef
2 cups chopped celery
1 cup chopped onion
1 cup chopped green pepper
2-3 garlic cloves, crushed
1 can (1 pound) tomatoes
1 can (8 ounces) tomato sauce

1 can (4 ounces) tomato paste
1 cup chunky peanut butter
2 cans (1 pound size) red kidney
    beans, drained
2-3 teaspoons chili powder
1 teaspoon ground cumin
1 teaspoon salt

Quick Method: Heat the peanut oil in a large skillet. Add and brown the beef, celery, onion, green pepper, and garlic. Stir in the remaining ingredients. Taste and add more salt if needed. Cover and simmer for 30 minutes. Add a little water if the chili is too thick.

Slow Method: This is preferable to the quick method both in convenience and tastiness — with the casserole in the oven, one is at ease and can attend to other matters. Heat the peanut oil in a large skillet. Add and brown the beef, celery, onion, green pepper, and garlic. Transfer to an oven-proof casserole and add all the remaining ingredients, except the kidney beans. Cover and bake in a slow (250°) oven for at least 4 hours. Add water if the chili becomes too thick. Add the kidney beans in the last hour.

The chili can be served plain or with rice, depending upon your preference. Serves 8 to 10

Beef Satay

1 pound lean beef (chuck or round), cut in 1-inch cubes
Peanut oil

SAUCE
1 tablespoon freshly ground coriander seeds
2 teaspoons ground fennel
2 teaspoons ground cumin
1 teaspoon chili powder
2 medium onions, chopped
1-2 cloves garlic, crushed

2 teaspoons shrimp paste or anchovy paste
2 tablespoons peanut oil
4-6 tablespoons peanut butter
1 cup coconut milk (see glossary)
¼ cup tamarind water (see glossary)
1 teaspoon sherry
1 teaspoon brown sugar
Salt to taste
Juice of 1 lemon

Make the satay sauce first. Combine the coriander, fennel, cumin, and chili powder, and fry with the onions, garlic, and fish paste in the 2 tablespoons of peanut oil. Add the peanut butter, coconut milk, tamarind water, sherry, sugar, and salt. Simmer 10 minutes and add the lemon juice.

Thread the beef cubes on skewers and broil, basting with peanut oil. Pour the satay sauce over the cubes and serve with raw, sliced cucumbers and boiled rice. Serves 4 to 6

Variation: substitute chicken for the beef.

Beef with Watercress

1 pound flank steak
2 egg whites
Salt
3 teaspoons cornstarch dissolved in 3 tablespoons water
2 teaspoons pepper oil (see glossary)
2 teaspoons minced ginger root
2 tablespoons finely chopped garlic
2 tablespoons chopped scallions

1 tablespoon chopped dried red chili pepper
6 tablespoons dry sherry
2 tablespoons dark soy sauce
2-3 teaspoons white vinegar
Sesame oil or peanut oil
½ teaspoon white pepper
2 teaspoons cayenne pepper
2-3 tablespoons peanut butter
¼ pound watercress (about one bunch) cut in 3-inch lengths

Cut the flank steak into 3- or 4-inch strips like carrot sticks. In a bowl, using your hands, mix the beef well with the egg whites, ¼ teaspoon salt, 2 teaspoons of the cornstarch-and-water mixture, and the pepper oil. Blend thoroughly.

In a bowl, combine 5 tablespoons of the sherry, the soy sauce, the remaining cornstarch-and-water mixture, the vinegar, 1½ teaspoons of sesame oil, and the white pepper.

In another small bowl, drench the cayenne thoroughly with sesame oil.

Heat the peanut butter in a wok or skillet until very hot. Add the watercress, the remaining sherry, and ¾ teaspoon of salt. Stir quickly for 3 to 5 minutes and remove to a serving dish.

In a clean wok or skillet, heat the peanut oil to approximately 300°. Add the beef strips and stir for about 15 seconds, until the strips are gray all over, then remove them from the oil.

In the same oil, cook the chili pepper until browned. Then return the beef to the wok with all the prepared ingredients, dry and liquid, except the cayenne–peanut oil mixture. After counting to two (while stirring), add the pepper mixture and continue stirring until the meat is barely browned outside and still quite rare inside. Then remove it from the wok with a slotted spoon and place it next to the watercress on the serving dish. Serve immediately. Serves 4

Fire Beef

*1 pound thinly sliced cooked beef,
    cut in strips*
10 tablespoons soy sauce
*1 tablespoon chopped sweet
    onion or leek*

1 tablespoon sugar
1 teaspoon peanut oil
1 teaspoon peanut butter
½ teaspoon chopped garlic
Salt and pepper to taste

Mix all the ingredients in a bowl and let stand for 10 minutes. Broil the beef, preferably on a charcoal fire, and serve immediately. This can be eaten like sukiyaki or served over rice. Serves 4 to 6

Beef and Fish Stew

2-3 medium onions
3 tablespoons peanut oil
1 pound chuck
2 pounds smoked fish (cod, mackerel, Boston blue, or whitefish)
4 tomatoes, chopped
6 okra

6 medium eggplants
6 cups beef stock
1 cup peanut butter
3-4 tablespoons water
1 teaspoon cayenne pepper
Pepper and salt to taste

Cut the beef into 1-inch cubes and the fish into small pieces. Slice the okra and peel and dice the eggplants.

Sauté the onions in the peanut oil. Add the fish and beef and fry over medium heat for several minutes. Reduce the heat and add the tomatoes, okra, eggplant, and stock. Mix the peanut butter with the water and add. Add pepper and salt. Simmer for 30 minutes. Serve with rice. Serves 6

Lamb Pilau

2 tablespoons olive oil
4 tablespoons peanut butter
4 cups water
2 teaspoons salt
½ teaspoon black pepper
2 pounds cooked lamb cut into
    ½-inch squares

¼ teaspoon chutney
½ pound cooking fat
2 onions, finely chopped
½ pound long-grain rice

Melt the olive oil in a large saucepan. Add the peanut butter and stir well; then add 2 cups of water, 1 teaspoon of salt, and the pepper. Boil for 2 to 3 minutes and stir in the meat. Cover and simmer gently for 6 to 8 minutes. Add the chutney.

In a separate pan, fry the onions in the fat until the onions are clear. Add the rice and continue to fry for an additional 5 minutes, stirring from time to time. Add the remaining teaspoon of salt and 2 cups of water, bring to a boil, and cook for 8 to 10 minutes. Add the lamb mixture and cook with the pan uncovered until all the liquid has been absorbed (approximately 5 minutes).

Serve with any or all of the following: mango chutney, grated coconut, grated green or red peppers. Serves 4

Variation: substitute cooked chicken for the lamb.

East Indian Lamb

½ cup grated coconut
5 tablespoons peanut oil
1 teaspoon nutmeg
10 cloves
1 teaspoon cinnamon
1 tablespoon freshly ground
  coriander seeds
Pinch of ground cumin
2 tablespoons chili powder
1 leaf lemon balm, preferably
  fresh (in summer)

1 tablespoon ground turmeric
2-3 tablespoons peanut butter
4 cloves garlic
2 onions
2 pounds lamb, cubed
3 ripe or canned tomatoes,
  peeled and chopped
3-4 cups coconut milk (see
  glossary)
Salt to taste

In a small saucepan, dry-fry the coconut until golden brown, then transfer it to a blender. Fry the nutmeg, cloves, cinnamon, coriander, and cumin in 2 tablespoons peanut oil for 1 to 2 minutes. Add them to the blender along with the chili powder, balm, turmeric, peanut butter, garlic, onions, and the remaining peanut oil. Blend into a fine paste. If necessary, to keep the blades turning, add a little extra peanut oil.

In a heavy skillet, combine the paste and the remaining ingredients, and simmer until tender, for approximately 1 hour. Serve over rice. Serves 6 to 8

Malayan Pork Satay

1 pound boneless pork loin
Salt and freshly ground black
   pepper to taste
1 cup coconut milk (see glossary)
2 teaspoons brown sugar
   SATAY SAUCE
1 clove garlic
1 small onion, chopped
¼ cup peanut butter

½ teaspoon ground dried red
   chili pepper
2 pieces preserved or candied
   ginger
1 tablespoon soy sauce
½ teaspoon salt
1 teaspoon ground turmeric
Juice of ½ lemon
1 scant cup water

Cut the pork into bite-sized cubes. Sprinkle with salt and pepper. Thread on skewers and marinate in the coconut milk at least 1 hour.

Next make the sauce. Put all the sauce ingredients in an electric blender and blend 30 seconds. Pour the sauce into the top part of a double boiler and bring to a boil over direct heat, stirring constantly. Place over boiling water and cook 30 minutes, stirring occasionally. Thin to desired consistency with more water or with coconut milk.

Drain the pork, sprinkle with the brown sugar, and barbecue or broil 15 to 20 minutes, turning frequently and basting often with coconut milk. Serve with the satay sauce and rice. Serves 4

Pork Satay in Peanut Butter Marinade

⅓ cup peanut butter

2 tablespoons coriander seeds

⅛ teaspoon cayenne pepper

¼ teaspoon freshly ground black
  pepper

1 clove garlic, finely chopped

2 tablespoons finely chopped
  onion

1 teaspoon salt

1 tablespoon brown sugar

3 tablespoons fresh lemon juice

¼ cup soy sauce

1½ pounds lean pork

Olive oil or melted butter

Mix all the ingredients, except the pork and olive oil in a large bowl.
Cut the pork into ½-inch cubes and add to the marinade. Mix well
and let stand 2 or 3 hours.

String the meat on skewers and broil slowly over a charcoal fire or
under a broiler flame, turning to brown on all sides. Cook 20 to 25
minutes or until the meat is well done. While cooking, baste often with
olive oil or butter. Serve hot. Serves 5 or 6

Pork with Peanut Butter Dip

MARINADE

1½ cups orange juice

Juice of 1 lemon

3 cloves garlic, chopped

½ teaspoon sugar

2 tablespoons soy sauce

Salt to taste

2 pounds boneless pork

   DIP

1 teaspoon butter

2 tablespoons peanut butter

1 teaspoon lemon juice

1 teaspoon cayenne pepper

¼ cup light cream

Combine the marinade ingredients in a large bowl, add the pork (cut into 1-inch cubes), and marinate it for at least 2 hours. Thread the meat on skewers and broil, preferably over a charcoal fire, for 15 to 20 minutes, or until cooked through and tender.

To make the dip, combine the butter, peanut butter, lemon juice, and pepper in a small saucepan, and simmer for 15 minutes. Add the cream, pour the dip into a bowl, and serve. Serves 6 to 8

Broiled Pork Kebab

½ cup dried apricots

1½ cups water

3 onions, diced

2 cloves garlic, chopped

¼ cup peanut or other vegetable
   oil

2-3 tablespoons peanut butter

3 tablespoons vinegar

¼-½ teaspoon cayenne pepper

1 crumbled bay leaf

2 teaspoons salt

2 tablespoons light brown sugar

3 tablespoons curry powder (see
   glossary)

½ cup beef gravy or stock

1 teaspoon black pepper

2 pounds boneless pork cut into
   1-inch cubes

Soak the apricots in the water overnight and cook slowly until soft. Puree the apricots and the liquid in a blender.

Sauté the onions and garlic in the peanut oil until transparent, soft, and golden brown; then add the peanut butter and cook until melted and blended. Add the sauté and all the remaining ingredients except the pork cubes to the apricot puree. Adjust the seasonings to achieve a tart, slightly hot flavor. Heat until the puree begins to bubble, pour it over the pork cubes, and marinate for at least 6 hours. Thread the meat on skewers and broil slowly for 20 to 30 minutes, turning and basting frequently with the marinade until crisp and brown.

Reheat the remaining marinade and place in a bowl. Serve the broiled pork cubes with steamed rice. Add marinade on top if desired. Serves 6

Pork Roast with Hot Peanut Sauce Crust

1 teaspoon butter
1 tablespoon peanut butter
1 tablespoon soy sauce
4 teaspoons lemon juice
1 teaspoon cayenne pepper
¼ cup cream or buttermilk

5-6 pounds pork rib cut from
the bone and tied
1-2 tablespoons star anise or
aniseed (see glossary)
1 teaspoon ground coriander

In a small saucepan, simmer the butter, peanut butter, soy sauce, 1 teaspoon of the lemon juice, and the cayenne for 15 minutes. Remove from the heat, cool slightly, blend in the cream or buttermilk, and reheat. Cool and let sit for at least 2 hours.

Coat the pork with the sauce and roll in the star anise and coriander. Pour the rest of the lemon juice over the meat and roast in moderate oven (350°), allowing 35 minutes to the pound. The sauce acts as a protective crust and keeps the juices in the meat. Serve with brown rice. Serves 10 to 12

Ham Puffs

2 eggs
½ cup peanut butter
½ cup ground cooked ham

1 teaspoon grated onion
Pinch of salt
1 cup cooked mashed potatoes

Separate 1 of the eggs, beat the yolk well, and mix with the peanut butter, ham, onion, and salt. Beat the white until stiff and fold into the peanut butter mixture.

Add the second egg to the mashed potatoes and mix thoroughly. Roll each teaspoon of ham mixture in mashed potato and bake on a greased cookie sheet in a moderate oven (350°) for 10 minutes. Serve hot. Makes 12 puffs and serves 4

Meat Loaf

1 medium onion, chopped
3 tablespoons peanut or other
  vegetable oil
1 pound ground beef
2-3 tablespoons peanut butter
¼ cup beef stock or buttermilk
1 stalk celery, diced

⅓ cup dried bread crumbs
1 egg
¼ cup chopped peanuts
Salt and pepper to taste
1 teaspoon chili powder
¼ teaspoon ground cumin
  (optional)

Sauté the onion in the oil until clear. Add the ground beef and cook until the pink is gone. Thin the peanut butter with the beef stock or buttermilk and add to the beef, along with the celery and bread crumbs. Add the egg, nuts, salt, pepper, chili powder, and cumin, and mix well. Turn into a greased 1-quart loaf pan and bake at 350° for 45 to 55 minutes. Serves 4 to 6

Variation: instead of 1 pound ground beef, use ½ pound ground beef mixed with ½ pound ground fresh pork.

CHICKEN

Chicken Curry

1 chicken, 3 to 3½ pounds
2 onions, finely sliced
4 cloves garlic, crushed
2 cloves
2-3 cardamon seeds, crushed
1 2-inch stick of cinnamon
¼ cup peanut oil
1 teaspoon ground coriander

½ teaspoon ground turmeric
½ teaspoon ground ginger
½ teaspoon ground cumin
½ teaspoon chili powder
2-3 tablespoons peanut butter
Salt to taste
Juice of ½ lemon

Skin the chicken and cut into 1-inch cubes. Fry the onions, garlic, cloves, cardamon, and cinnamon in the peanut oil. When the onions are golden brown, add the curry ingredients, that is, the coriander, turmeric, ginger, cumin, and chili, as well as the peanut butter and salt, and cook over low heat for 5 minutes. Add the pieces of chicken and brown, stirring occasionally to prevent burning.

Add enough water to form a thick gravy. Cover the skillet and simmer until the chicken is tender (30 to 40 minutes). Remove the cinnamon stick. Squeeze lemon juice over the curry just before serving. Serve with rice. Serves 6

Chicken in Peanut Butter Sauce

1 fresh red chili pepper or
  1 teaspoon dried red pepper
  flakes
Meat of ½ medium-sized chicken
2 tablespoons oil
2 medium onions. chopped
6 sliced ripe tomatoes or *1 can*
  (1 pound) undrained tomatoes

⅓ cup peanut butter
2 tablespoons tamari or *soy sauce*
  (see glossary)
2 cloves garlic
1 cup cooked brown rice

Peel and chop the chili pepper. This is made easier by coating with a little oil and broiling for 2 minutes. Remove the skin and chop.

Fry the chicken in the oil for 4 to 5 minutes before adding the onions. Cook the onions until clear and tender. Add the tomatoes, cover, lower heat, and simmer for half an hour. Stir in the remaining ingredients. Simmer several minutes longer. Serve on brown rice. Serves 4

Chicken Satay

3 whole chicken breasts,
  boned and skinned
1 cup coconut milk (see glossary)
1 clove garlic, crushed
½ teaspoon salt
¼ teaspoon freshly ground
  white pepper

¼ cup peanut butter
2 small fresh red chili peppers,
  seeded and chopped, or *2*
  teaspoons dried red pepper
  flakes

Slice the chicken into bite-sized strips ½ inch wide by 1 inch long. Pour the coconut milk into a bowl, add the garlic, salt, and pepper, and marinate the chicken slices in the liquid at room temperature for 2 to 3 hours.

Preheat a broiler. Thread the chicken slices on individual metal or wooden skewers. Broil 3 to 4 inches from the source of the heat, turning two or three times, for about 10 minutes, or until the chicken is tender.

Place the marinade and peppers into the container of an electric blender. Blend at high speed for 30 seconds. Heat and serve as a dipping sauce for the chicken strips. Serves 6

Oriental Chicken Kebabs

6 chicken breasts, boned
⅔ cup soy sauce
¼ cup sherry
2-3 tablespoons peanut butter

1 clove garlic, crushed
1 tablespoon grated dried
  ginger root
½ teaspoon sugar

Cut the chicken meat into large cubes and marinate in the remaining ingredients for 2 to 3 hours. Thread the meat on skewers and broil briefly on all sides over high heat. Serves 6

Hacked Chicken

1 pound boned chicken breasts
3-4 tablespoons peanut butter
1 cup peanut oil
2 tablespoons soy sauce
2 tablespoons white vinegar
2 teaspoons cayenne pepper
2 teaspoons minced ginger root

1½ teaspoons finely chopped
  scallions
2-3 cloves garlic, chopped
2 teaspoons ground coriander
  seeds
2-3 teaspoons pepper oil (see
  glossary)

Plunge the chicken into boiling water and let it stand for 5 minutes.

Remove, drain, cool, skin, and pull into strips about 3 inches long, ¼ inch wide and ¼ inch thick.

In a large bowl, combine the peanut butter with 1 tablespoon peanut oil, and mix until smooth. Stir in the soy sauce and vinegar.

In a small dish, moisten the cayenne thoroughly with the remaining peanut oil. Add to the peanut butter mixture along with the ginger, scallions, garlic, coriander, and pepper oil. Mix well, then transfer to a 2-quart saucepan and bring to a boil. Add the chicken and simmer for 20 minutes. The chicken can be served hot or cold. Serves 4 to 6

Sweet and Sour Chicken

¼ cup soy sauce

1 chicken, 3-3½ pounds, cut into
   serving pieces

¼ cup peanut oil

3-4 tablespoons peanut butter

⅓ cup pineapple juice

⅓ cup water

1 cup canned pineapple chunks

½ cup sliced green pepper

2 tablespoons cornstarch

⅓ cup vinegar

Pour the soy sauce over the chicken and place in the refrigerator for an hour. Drain and reserve the liquid.

In a large skillet, heat the oil and brown the chicken. Arrange in an ovenproof dish.

In a saucepan, combine the vinegar, pineapple juice, peanut butter, and water and bring to a boil. Pour the sauce over the chicken and bake at 350° for 45 to 50 minutes. Add the pineapple chunks and green pepper, and bake 10 minutes more.

Place the chicken on a serving platter. Pour the sauce into a saucepan, add the cornstarch, and cook on the top of the stove until the sauce is thickened, stirring constantly. Pour the sauce over the chicken. Serve with rice. Serves 4

FISH AND SHELLFISH

Stuffed Bass

1 small sea bass, 5-7 pounds
2 tablespoons peanut oil
1 sliced onion
1 teaspoon ground coriander
½ teaspoon cumin seeds
3 tablespoons peanut butter
1 teaspoon anchovy paste or
   shrimp paste

1 leaf fresh lemon balm, in season,
   or ½ teaspoon lemon juice
1 teaspoon brown sugar
1 cup coconut milk (see glossary)
Salt to taste

Scale the fish, taking care not to damage the skin. Ideally, the fish should be rubbed hard until the backbone is released from the rest of the flesh and is then pulled out through a gill opening. Then the flesh is pulled out through the same opening, and the entrails discarded, leaving the skin whole but empty. If you think you will not be able

to do this, split the fish along one side, remove bones and flesh, and sew up after stuffing.

Remove the fish from the bones and flake the flesh with your fingers.

Heat the oil, add the onion, and fry until golden brown. Add the coriander, cumin, peanut butter, and fish paste. Then grind together with the remaining ingredients and fish flesh until smooth.

Fill the fish skin with the mixture, wrap in greased aluminum foil, and broil 20 minutes in the oven or over charcoal. Serves 8

Poached Mackerel

1 whole mackerel, 1½ to 2 pounds
1 large onion, grated
1 tablespoon ground dried red
  chili pepper
3 cloves garlic, crushed

3-4 tablespoons peanut butter
½ lemon, thinly sliced
3-4 basil leaves, preferably fresh
Salt to taste

Blend the onion, chili pepper, garlic, and peanut butter into a paste. Coat the fish and add the lemon slices and basil. Place in a shallow pan or Chinese wok, and add water to cover the fish. Simmer over a low fire, without stirring, until the fish is cooked (15 to 25 minutes). Serves 3

Fried Fish with Vinegar and Peanut Butter

4 mackerel, cod, or flounder fillets
3 tablespoons peanut oil
1 teaspoon ground coriander
¼ cup cider vinegar
¼ cup peanut butter
½ teaspoon ground dry mustard

GARNISH
½ teaspoon ground cumin
1 teaspoon ground coriander
½ teaspoon cinnamon
¼ cup chopped walnuts

Wash the fillets, pat dry, and dip in flour. In a large skillet, heat the oil and fry the fillets until golden brown on both sides.

In a small bowl, mix the coriander, vinegar, peanut butter, and mustard until a medium-thick mixture is obtained. Pour on the bottom of a serving dish, add the fried fish, and pour the oil from the frying pan over it. Garnish with the ground cumin, ground coriander, ground cinnamon, and walnuts. Eat hot or cold. Serves 4

Shrimp Satay

1 pound large raw shrimp, shelled and deveined
1 tablespoon peanut or other vegetable oil
1 clove garlic, crushed
½ teaspoon anchovy paste
1 tablespoon grated lemon peel or

1 leaf fresh lemon balm
1 teaspoon ground dried red chili pepper
½ cup peanut butter
½ cup coconut milk (see glossary)
1 tablespoon lemon juice

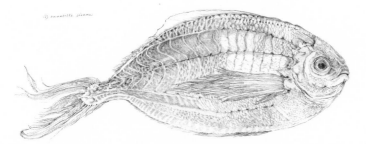

Heat the oil, add the garlic and anchovy paste, and stir until the paste is well blended. Add the remaining ingredients, except the shrimp, and stir together.

Thread the shrimp on skewers, coat with the peanut butter sauce, and broil 5 minutes on each side. Recoat with sauce if necessary. Serves 4 (three shrimp each)

RICE AND PASTA

Indonesian Rice

NASI GORENG

1 chicken breast	2-3 tablespoons peanut butter
½ pound shrimp	1 teaspoon ground coriander
¼ pound cooked ham	½ teaspoon ground cumin
1 fresh sweet pepper	¼ teaspoon ground anise
1 fresh green chili pepper	6 cups steamed rice
3 onions, thinly sliced	3 eggs, lightly beaten
2 cloves garlic, crushed	¼ cup water
6 tablespoons peanut oil	Salt and pepper to taste

Bone the chicken breast and devein the shrimp; cut both into small pieces. Tear the ham into strips. Cut the peppers into strips.

Sauté the onions and garlic in 2 tablespoons of the peanut oil until the onions are clear and tender. Combine the peanut butter and the chicken cubes, then add them to the onions and garlic. Cook over high heat for 5 minutes, stirring constantly. Simmer the coriander, cumin, and anise together for 10 minutes with a little water and add to the chicken mixture. Then add the shrimp and continue to simmer for 8 to 10 minutes. Add the rice and heat.

In a small skillet, combine 2 tablespoons of the peanut oil, the eggs, water, salt, and pepper, and add half the mixture to the skillet; cook until set. Remove and cut into strips. Repeat with the rest of the mixture.

Fry the chili pepper strips in the 2 remaining tablespoons of peanut oil until tender and remove them from the skillet. Then add the sweet-pepper strips, fry them until tender, and remove them also. Last, separate the rest of the onion into rings and fry until lightly browned.

Place the rice mixture in the center of a serving dish. Ring with egg strips. Top with the ham, fried peppers, and onion rings. Serves 6

Rice with Chilies

1 cup peanut butter
2 cups milk
1 can (¼ ounce) green chilies, chopped
2 teaspoons chili powder
½ teaspoon salt
¼ teaspoon ginger
1-2 cloves garlic, crushed

3 tablespoons chopped parsley
3½ cups cooked rice
4 ounces cheddar cheese, shredded
GARNISH
Chopped parsley
Green pepper strips

Blend the peanut butter and milk until smooth, and add the chilies, chili powder, salt, ginger, garlic, and parsley.

Place half the rice in a buttered 2-quart casserole. Pour half the chili mixture on top. Add the remaining rice and top with the chili mixture.

Bake in a 375° oven for 30 minutes, then remove from oven, top with the cheddar cheese, and bake for an additional 8 to 10 minutes. Garnish with the parsley and peppers. Serves 6 to 8

Peanut Butter Cutlets

½ cup peanut butter　　　　*Salt and pepper to taste*
1 cup well-boiled rice　　　*¼ cup grated sharp cheddar*
2 eggs　　　　　　　　　　　*cheese*
½ cup tomato puree

Mix all the ingredients into a stiff paste in a saucepan. Shape into cutlets. Roll in seasoned flour, beaten egg, and bread crumbs, and fry. Serve with cooked vegetables. Serves 4

Peanut Butter and Rice Loaf

This is very much like the peanut butter cutlets, though the texture is smoother.

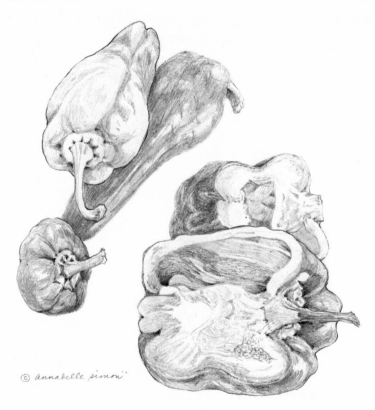

© annabelle simon

1 medium onion, chopped	*1 cup bread crumbs, soaked in*
2-3 tablespoons vegetable oil,	*at least 1 cup milk*
preferably peanut oil	*1 egg*
1 cup cooked rice, preferably	*Salt to taste*
brown rice	*¼ teaspoon powdered mustard*
1 cup peanut butter	*½ teaspoon black pepper*

Sauté the onion until golden brown and combine with the remaining ingredients. Grease a 9x5x3-inch loaf pan and pack in the mixture. Bake for 45 to 50 minutes in a 350° oven.

Turn out on a hot serving platter, slice, and serve with either a sharp cheese sauce made with mustard or a mushroom sauce. Serves 6 to 8

Brown Rice with Peanut Butter and Bananas

2 cups brown rice

4 cups water

2 cups tomato juice

2 onions, chopped

2 green peppers, chopped

½ cup peanut oil

1 tablespoon curry powder

(see glossary)

Salt and pepper to taste

3 tomatoes

½ cup peanut butter

2 bananas, sliced in rounds

Cook the rice in the water and tomato juice. Sauté the onions and peppers in ¼ cup of the peanut oil. Add the curry, salt, and pepper, then ¼ cup water, the tomatoes and the peanut butter. Cook 5 minutes. Fry the bananas separately in the rest of the oil. Pour the sauce over the rice and top with the bananas. Serves 6 to 8

Spaghetti with Pepperoni–Peanut Butter Sauce

½ pound spaghetti
3 tablespoons oil
1 small onion, sliced
1 clove garlic, minced
*1-1½ cups pepperoni or other
  very spicy sausage, sliced ¼"
  thick*

1 can (6 ounces) tomato paste
Salt and pepper to taste
1 bay leaf
¼ teaspoon oregano
½ cup peanut butter

Cook the spaghetti in rapidly boiling salted water with 1 table-spoon of the oil.

In a separate skillet, heat the remaining oil, add the onion, garlic, and pepperoni, and saute for 2 minutes or until the onion is transparent. Add all the other ingredients except the peanut butter and bring to a boil; then add the peanut butter, cover, and simmer over low heat for 20 minutes. Pour over the cooked spaghetti. Serves 4

VEGETABLES

Vegetables with Peanut Butter and Coconut Milk Sauce

GADO-GADO

SAUCE

3 tablespoons vegetable oil

½ onion, finely chopped

1 clove garlic, chopped

1 teaspoon shrimp paste
(optional)

2 cups water

2 cups peanut butter

3 tablespoons light brown sugar

1 tablespoon finely chopped fresh
red chili pepper, or 1 teaspoon
dried red pepper flakes

2 bay leaves

½ teaspoon grated ginger root

1 teaspoon salt

4 cups coconut milk (see
glossary)

¼ cup tamarind water (see
glossary)

VEGETABLES

1 pound fresh uncooked spinach,
coarsely chopped

2 fresh bean curd cakes

1 pound new potatoes, boiled
and then fried

1 pound sliced steamed
   string beans
1 pound fresh bean sprouts or
   2 cups canned sprouts

1 cup shredded iceberg lettuce
2 unpeeled cucumbers, sliced
   crosswise
2 sliced hard-boiled eggs

Cook the onion and garlic in the oil over moderate heat until the onions are soft and transparent. Add the shrimp paste and blend. Add the water and bring to a boil. Then add the peanut butter, brown sugar, chilies, bay leaves, ginger root, and salt. Reduce the heat to low and add the coconut milk and tamarind water. Simmer approximately 15 minutes until the sauce holds its shape lightly. Adjust the seasoning. Cool to room temperature.

Serve over a mixture of the raw and cooked vegetables. Arrange the spinach and bean curd in the center and around it place the potatoes, beans, bean sprouts, lettuce, cucumbers, and eggs. Serves 8

Mixed Hot Vegetables

6-8 carrots
1 eggplant
1 pound cabbage
½ pound string beans
3 cucumbers
2 quarts boiling water
1 tablespoon ground turmeric
6 cloves garlic, finely chopped

3 onions, finely chopped
6 small fresh red chili peppers,
   chopped
1 tablespoon anchovy paste
½ cup peanut butter
2 cups vegetable oil

2 cups wine vinegar   *2 tablespoons sugar*
⅓ teaspoon salt

Cut vegetables into 2-inch strips and lightly blanch separately in the boiling water.

In a mixing bowl, blend turmeric, onion, garlic, peppers, anchovy paste, and peanut butter. Heat ½ cup oil in a frying pan or wok, and fry the mixture for 5 minutes.

Add the remaining oil, vinegar, salt and sugar and bring to a boil. Put in the vegetables one at a time and stir lightly. Simmer only until vegetables are barely tender. Serve with rice. As a luncheon dish, serves 6 to 8

Peanut Butter Burgers

Start with the recipe for vegetarian chopped chicken liver (page 14); then add 1 egg and enough seasoned bread crumbs to make a thick mixture. Form into four patties.

Heat 2 to 3 tablespoons vegetable oil and fry the patties in a skillet over a moderate heat until they are lightly browned on both sides. Serves 4

Spinach

1 pound fresh spinach	*2-3 tablespoons soy sauce*
½ cup peanut oil	*2-3 tablespoons peanut butter*
¼ cup chopped onion	*Salt and cayenne pepper to taste*
1 chopped tomato	

Wash the spinach and remove the stems. Shake out the excess moisture and steam in a covered pot until tender.

Heat ¼ cup of the peanut oil in a large skillet and sauté the onion and tomato until tender. Remove them from the oil and keep them warm in another pan.

Add the remaining oil to the skillet and stir in the soy sauce, cayenne, and peanut butter. Cook over low heat, stirring constantly, until the liquid thickens. Add the spinach, tomato, and onion. Adjust the seasoning. Serves 4

Broccoli

1 bunch broccoli
2 tablespoons butter
¼ cup onion
¼ pound mushrooms
1 tablespoon flour
½ cup half-and-half

½ cup shredded cheddar cheese
1 egg
1 teaspoon salt
¼ teaspoon pepper
3 tablespoons peanut butter

Cook the broccoli until tender. Drain.

In a saucepan, melt the butter over moderate heat. Sauté the onions and mushrooms until clear and tender. Add the flour and mix thoroughly. Gradually add the half-and-half to make a white sauce. Add the remaining ingredients.

Place the broccoli in a 1-quart buttered casserole and pour the sauce over it. Bake at 350° for 40 minutes. Serves 4

Potato Pancakes

2 eggs
2 tablespoons Annabelle's Peanut
  Butter Dip (page 5) or

1 tablespoon peanut butter and
1 clove garlic, crushed
2 large potatoes

¼ teaspoon salt

⅛ teaspoon pepper

Finely ground bread crumbs

4 tablespoons vegetable oil

Place the eggs, peanut butter dip, potatoes, salt, and pepper in that order into a blender and mix until well blended. Remove from the blender and add enough bread crumbs to make a mixture thick enough to hold together in a tablespoon.

In a large skillet, heat the vegetable oil until it begins to ripple when shifted, add individual tablespoonfuls of the mixture, and cook until golden brown on both sides. Add extra oil as needed. Serves 4 (three pancakes apiece)

Sweet Potatoes

2 cups mashed sweet potatoes

* (1 pound fresh or canned)*

⅓ cup orange or pineapple juice

3 tablespoons peanut butter

¼ cup brown sugar

½ teaspoon salt

6 slices fried bacon crumbled

* into small pieces*

2 tablespoons melted butter or

* margarine*

Mix all the ingredients. Grease a glass baking dish and fill with the mixture. Cover with additional bacon slices or marshmallows. Bake 30 minutes in a 350° oven. Serves 6

Stuffed Tomatoes

4 tomatoes

½ cup cooked rice

2-3 tablespoons peanut butter

½ teaspoon salt

2 tablespoons minced onion

¼ cup chopped celery

Pinch of cayenne pepper

Slice off the tops of the tomatoes. Scoop out the pulp, chop, and mix with the remaining ingredients.

Fill the tomato shells with the mixture and bake in a shallow oven-proof dish at 375° for 30 minutes. Serves 4

Variation: ½ cup of bread that has been soaked in water and the excess squeezed out may be substituted for the rice. The inner texture will be altered but the taste will be similar.

Braised Celery

1 medium onion, sliced

3-4 tablespoons vegetable oil

3 cups sliced celery

½ cup water

3 tablespoons peanut butter

2 tablespoons soy sauce

Pinch of cayenne pepper

Salt to taste

In a skillet, sauté the onions lightly in the oil. Add the celery and water, bring to a boil, and simmer until tender (5 to 8 minutes). Drain, reserving the liquid, and set aside. Stir the remaining ingredients into the liquid, thin (if necessary) with 3 or 4 tablespoons of water, and pour over the celery. Serves 4 to 6

Ugandan Peanut Butter Stew

3 tablespoons oil
2 onions, chopped
4 cloves garlic, pressed
2 carrots, diced
1 cauliflower, cut into small pieces
6-8 tomatoes, sliced, or 1 can
* (1 pound) tomatoes, including*
* the liquid*

½ cup peanut butter
½ cup water
1 teaspoon chili powder
½ teaspoon cayenne pepper
Salt to taste

Heat the oil in a skillet and sauté the onions and garlic. Add the carrots and cauliflower and continue to cook. After 2 or 3 minutes add the tomatoes, cover, lower the heat, and simmer for 30 minutes. Then add the peanut butter, water, and seasonings. Cook 5 to 10 minutes more. Serve with brown rice or millet. Serves 4

Potato Salad

½ cup mayonnaise

¼ cup vinegar

3-4 tablespoons peanut butter

1 teaspoon salt

¼ teaspoon pepper

½ teaspoon dry mustard

4 medium-sized cooked potatoes,
   diced

1 cup sliced celery

½ onion, diced

Combine the peanut butter, mayonnaise, and vinegar, and blend well. Add the salt, pepper, and mustard. Mix the potatoes, celery, and onion together, add the mayonnaise mixture, and toss lightly. Serves 4 to 6

SALAD DRESSINGS AND SAUCES

Peanut Butter Salad Dressing I

¼ cup wine vinegar
¼ cup salad oil
Pinch of cayenne or black pepper
Pinch of dry mustard

2 tablespoons peanut butter
1 tablespoon light rum
1 clove garlic
Salt to taste

Blend all ingredients together in a blender until well mixed and serve over raw vegetables. If you are using a rotary beater, put the garlic through a press beforehand. Makes about ¾ cup

Peanut Butter Salad Dressing II

2 tablespoons peanut butter
½ cup oil

2 tablespoons tamari or soy sauce
(see glossary)

2 tablespoons lemon juice   2 cloves garlic, pressed

Blend all the ingredients. The dressing goes well with avocado. Makes about 1 cup

Sauce for Beef Fondue

½ cup peanut butter   1 cup dashi (see glossary)
½ cup soy sauce   1 tablespoon dry red wine

Combine all the ingredients and serve. Makes 2 cups

Peanut Butter Sambal

2-3 tablespoons peanut butter   1 lemon or lime leaf, or 1 leaf
1 teaspoon shrimp paste or   fresh lemon balm
 anchovy paste   Salt to taste
½-1 fresh hot green or red chili   Soy sauce to taste (optional)
 pepper

Place all the ingredients in a blender or in a mortar and blend until smooth. The sambal can be added to many dishes, but it is especially good in rice or chicken broth. Makes ¼ to ½ cup

Rouille

2 medium potatoes, boiled and
  mashed
3 cloves garlic
3 egg yolks
½ teaspoon paprika

½ teaspoon ground saffron
1 cup peanut butter
1 cup heavy cream
Salt and pepper to taste

Place the potatoes, garlic, egg yolks, paprika, and saffron in a blender, and blend well. Mix the peanut butter and cream together and gradually add to the potato mixture while blending at a low speed. Season with salt and pepper. The mixture should have the consistency of mayonnaise. Serve as an accompaniment to thick fish soups, such as bouillabaisse, or with poached fish. Makes 3 cups

Peanut-Coconut Garnish

1 cup grated dried coconut
1 teaspoon ground cumin
½ tablespoon brown sugar
1 medium onion, minced
2 cloves garlic, pressed

1 small slice green ginger (see
  glossary)
1 tablespoon tamarind water (see
  glossary)
1 teaspoon lemon juice

¼-½ *cup peanut butter*   ¼ *cup peanuts*
Peanut or other vegetable oil

Combine all the ingredients except the peanuts and fry over low heat in a small amount of oil until the mixture is golden brown. Cool and stir in the peanuts. Serve as an accompaniment to curry dishes. Makes about 2 cups

CEREALS, BREADS
AND SANDWICHES

Peanut Granola

8-10 cups rolled oats
1 cup sesame seeds
1 cup dried coconut, grated
1 cup roasted soybeans
1 cup whole-wheat flour
1 tablespoon salt
1 teaspoon vanilla
2 teaspoons cinnamon

½ cup honey
½ cup light molasses
½ cup oil
½ cup peanut butter
½ cup water
1 cup raisins
1 cup whole or slivered almonds

Combine all the dry ingredients except the raisins. Combine the rest of the ingredients in a saucepan and cook over low heat, stirring constantly, until the butter melts and all the ingredients are blended. Pour the liquid over the dry ingredients and toss well. Bake the mixture in an oiled baking pan in a 325° oven until browned (approximately 20 minutes). Add the raisins. Store in a covered container.

High-Protein Breakfast Puree

2 cups milk
1 cup peanut butter
1 egg, well beaten

1 tablespoon sugar
½ teaspoon salt

Blend the milk and peanut butter in a saucepan and bring to a boil over low heat, stirring constantly. Add the remaining ingredients and again bring to a boil. The mixture should have the consistency of medium cream. Add more milk if necessary. Serve immediately as is, or over cornflakes or another crisp dry cereal. Serves 4

Yeast Bread

1 cup milk
1 cake or package dry yeast
¼ cup warm water
1 tablespoon sugar

3½ cups sifted flour
¼ cup peanut butter
1 egg
1½ teaspoons salt

Scald and cool the milk. Dissolve the yeast in the water. In a mixing bowl, add the milk to the sugar and 2 cups of the flour. Stir in the yeast. Cover and set aside until bubbly. Mix the peanut butter, egg, and salt, and add to the sponge. Stir in the remaining flour.

Turn the dough out onto a lightly floured board and knead for 10 minutes. Place in a greased bowl, cover, and let rise until double in size. (In the wintertime, place in a cool oven with a bowl of steaming hot water underneath it.)

Punch down and let rise until double in size again. Shape into a loaf and place in a baking pan. Let rise until double in size. Bake 30 minutes in a 350° oven. Makes 1 loaf

Whole-Wheat Bread

1½ cups whole-wheat pastry
    flour
⅓ cup powdered milk
1 teaspoon salt
2 teaspoons double-acting baking
    powder

¾ cup peanut butter
1¼ cups milk (sweet or sour), or
    buttermilk, or yoghurt
⅓ cup honey or dark molasses
½ cup wheat germ

Into a mixing bowl, sift the flour, milk, salt, and baking powder. Add the rest of the ingredients and stir vigorously for 1 minute. Line the bottom of a loaf pan with heavy paper and grease well. Pour the batter into the pan, forcing it into the corners. Make an indentation lengthwise through the center and bake it at 350° for 45 minutes. Makes 1 loaf

Peanut Bread

2 cups sifted all-purpose flour
3 teaspoons double-acting baking
   powder
1 1/4 teaspoons salt
1/3 cup sugar

1 teaspoon grated orange rind
1 cup peanut butter
2 eggs, slightly beaten
1 1/4 cups milk
1/2 cup chopped peanuts

Sift together the flour, baking powder, salt, and sugar. Add the orange rind and mix thoroughly. Cut in the peanut butter with two knives or rub it in with the finger tips. Combine the eggs and milk, add to the dry ingredients, and stir just enough to moisten. Add the peanuts and pour the mixture into a 9x5x3-inch loaf pan. Bake in a moderate oven (350°) for about 1 hour and 10 minutes. Makes 1 loaf

Baking Powder Biscuits

1 1/2 cups whole-wheat pastry
   flour
1 1/4 teaspoons salt
1/4 cup powdered milk
4 teaspoons double-acting baking
   powder

1/2 cup wheat germ
1 tablespoon honey
1/4 cup peanut butter
2 tablespoons vegetable oil
3/4 cup milk (sweet or sour), or
   buttermilk, or yoghurt

Sift the dry ingredients into a mixing bowl. Cut in the honey, peanut butter, and oil. Then add the milk and stir vigorously for half a minute. Turn the dough out onto a floured canvas and knead for 3 minutes.

© annabelle simon cohn 1974

Pat down to 1-inch thickness and cut out the biscuits with a cutter. Place them close together on a greased baking sheet and bake at 450° for 12 to 15 minutes. Makes 18 to 24 biscuits

Variation: instead of the whole-wheat flour, use soy, rye, or buck-wheat flour, and knead 5 minutes.

Luncheon Sandwiches

Peanut butter, crumbled fried bacon, and grated peeled apple, mixed together and spread on cracked-wheat bread. The sandwiches can be served as such or grilled until the peanut butter melts.

Peanut butter and ham with mayonnaise and mustard on rye bread.

Peanut butter and mayonnaise blended, spread on whole-wheat bread, and topped with grated raw carrot.

Fried bacon, peanut butter, and pickle relish on white bread and grilled.

Cream cheese, peanut butter, and pickle relish on pumpernickel bread.

Cream cheese, peanut butter, crushed garlic, and salt on pumper-nickel or sour-dough rye bread.

Cream cheese, peanut butter, horseradish, and chopped capers on pumpernickel. Horseradish and capers can be replaced by chopped olives.

Peanut butter, tomato, and chopped green onion on cracked wheat, grilled.

Salami, peanut butter, and thinly sliced onion on rye bread.

Spicy Sloppy Joes made with a sauté of chopped onion, chopped garlic, ground chuck, peanut butter, tomato sauce, crumbled oregano, salt, and Tabasco sauce, and served on crusty rolls.

Frankfurters, split and placed skin side down on a grill. Top them with cheese, relish, chopped onion, and peanut butter, and grill them until the cheese and peanut butter are melted. Stuff into warm hot-dog buns and serve at once.

Apple or mango chutney, cream cheese, and peanut butter on San Francisco sour-dough rye.

Tea Sandwiches

Peanut butter, banana, and honey on raisin bread or toasted white bread.

Peanut butter and marshmallows or Marshmallow Fluff grilled on white bread or saltine crackers.

Peanut butter and grated apple on Anadama bread.

Orange juice concentrate (1 part) or orange marmalade blended with peanut butter (2 parts) on toast.

Peanut butter, honey, crumbled bacon, wheat germ, and crushed drained pineapple on toast.

Chopped pitted dates, peanut butter, a little lemon juice, and mayonnaise on cracked-wheat bread.

Cooked apricots and peanut butter on toast.

Raisins, shredded carrots, peanut butter, and salad dressing on Anadama bread.

DESSERTS AND ICE CREAM

Peanutty-Chocolate Apple Dessert

4 tablespoons butter
¼ cup white shortening
Grated rind of 1 lemon
1 tablespoon ice water
1 tablespoon bourbon whiskey
1 cup sifted flour
Pinch of salt
4 ounces semisweet chocolate
3 tablespoons peanut butter
3 tablespoons water
1½ teaspoons vanilla

3 medium baking apples, peeled
 and sliced
⅓ cup orange marmalade
⅓ cup apricot jam
¼ cup raisins
1 egg yolk
2 tablespoons sour cream
1 teaspoon sugar
Sweetened whipped cream for
 garnishing

Preheat the oven to 450°. Cream the butter and shortening together in an electric blender. Beat in the lemon rind, ice water, and whiskey. Reduce the speed to slow and gradually add the flour and salt.

Spoon the mixture into a lightly greased 9-inch pie dish. Bake 15 to 20 minutes until crisp and golden. Remove from the oven and allow to cool in the pan.

Reduce the oven heat to 350°.

In the top of a double boiler, combine the chocolate, peanut butter, water, and 1 teaspoon of the vanilla. Cook over hot water until melted. Spread the mixture over the crust in the pie dish. Allow to cool.

Place the apples, marmalade, jam, and raisins in a saucepan and heat slowly. When hot, gently stir until blended. Pour this mixture into the pie dish.

Beat the egg yolk with the sour cream, sugar, and the remaining vanilla. Spread this over the pie. Bake 5 to 10 minutes, until the top is set. The dessert will still have a loose consistency. Cool and serve with sweetened whipped cream. Serves 6 to 8

Bananas with Rum

4 ripe bananas
3 tablespoons peanut butter

3 tablespoons brown sugar
⅓ cup light rum

Preheat the oven to 350°.

Halve the bananas lengthwise and arrange in a shallow baking dish. Dot with the peanut butter and sprinkle with the sugar. Bake for approximately 20 minutes.

Warm the rum. Do not let it boil. Pour it over the bananas and ignite. Serves 4

Peanut Butter Soufflé

1 envelope unflavored gelatin	*½ teaspoon ginger*
3 tablespoons peanut butter	*4 egg whites*
½ cup brown sugar	*½ cup granulated sugar*
1 cup orange juice concentrate	*1 cup heavy cream, whipped*
¼ teaspoon salt	GARNISH
4 egg yolks	*¼ cup peanuts or candied fruit*

In a saucepan, dissolve the gelatin in 2 tablespoons of warm water. Add the peanut butter, brown sugar, orange juice, salt, and egg yolks, and stir until blended. Cook over low heat, stirring constantly, until the peanut butter is melted. Allow to cool. Add the ginger.

Beat the egg whites to soft peaks. Gradually add the granulated sugar until the egg whites are in stiff peaks. Fold the egg whites into the peanut butter mixture. Whip the cream and fold it in.

Wrap a waxed-paper collar around a 1½-quart soufflé dish or a round bowl with straight sides so that the collar protrudes 2 inches above the rim. Pour the mixture into the dish, to the top of the collar. Chill until firm, remove the collar, and garnish. Serves 6 to 8

Custard

2 cups light cream
2 cups milk
1 cup peanut butter
¾ cup light-brown sugar

½ teaspoon ginger
¼ cup rice flour or cornstarch
2 tablespoons peanuts, finely
  chopped

In a medium saucepan, combine the cream, 1½ cups of the milk, the peanut butter, sugar, and ginger, and bring to a boil. Remove from the heat and let stand for 20 minutes. Strain the mixture through a fine sieve set over a bowl.

In the same saucepan, dissolve the rice flour or cornstarch in the remaining milk. Add the peanut butter mixture and cook over low heat for 20 minutes, stirring constantly. The custard should have thickened sufficiently to coat a spoon lightly. Strain again, spoon the custard into individual bowls, and chill. Serves 6

Peanut Butter Syllabub

3-4 tablespoons peanut butter
2-3 tablespoons ginger brandy
1 cup whipping cream

½ cup light-brown sugar
Grated nutmeg

Blend the peanut butter and brandy and set aside. Beat the cream until it begins to firm. Add the sugar and beat until the mixture begins to peak. Add the peanut butter and brandy, and mix until smooth. Serve in individual dessert dishes and top with nutmeg. Serves 4

Peanut Butter Roll

7 eggs, separated	*4 ounces shelled peanuts*
1 cup sugar	*2 cups heavy cream*
1 teaspoon baking powder	*Confectioners' sugar*
¼ teaspoon almond extract	*1 teaspoon vanilla extract*

Grind the peanuts in a Mouli or other nut grinder (not a blender) to produce ½ cup of ground nuts.

Butter the bottom and sides of an 11½x17½-inch jelly roll pan. Cover the pan with a sheet of wax paper cut 4 inches or so wider and longer than the pan. Push the paper down tightly against the bottom and sides of the pan. Butter the top of the paper.

Preheat the oven to 350°.

Beat the egg yolks together and then gradually beat the sugar into them. Continue beating until the mixture is smooth and turns almost white. Next beat in the baking powder, almond extract, and finally, the ground peanuts.

In another bowl, beat the egg whites until they form stiff peaks. Stir a little of the whites into the yolk mixture to lighten it. Then pour the yolk mixture into the whites. Fold in until the whites no longer show.

Pour the batter into the prepared pan. Tilt the pan back and forth until the batter is spread uniformly over the surface. Bake in a pre-heated oven for 18 to 20 minutes, or until the tip of a knife stuck into the center comes out clean. Remove from the oven, cover with wax paper, and then with a dry kitchen towel. Let cool completely.

Whip the cream, flavor it with confectioners' sugar to taste (2 to 3 tablespoons should do it), and add the vanilla.

Gently remove the towel and wax paper from the peanut roll. Sprinkle with confectioners' sugar and turn out (invert) onto a triple layer of wax paper.

Set the serving dish you intend to use at one end of the triple wax paper, ready to receive the finished roll. Trim off the crusty edges of the roll and spoon the whipped cream on top.

To roll up, grasp the corners of the near end of the wax paper and use them like handles to start rolling the peanut butter roll away from you into the serving dish. Speed is not of the essence. Roughly two and a half turns should completely roll up the roll and leave it sitting pretty on the dish, seam side down. After the first turn, the roll will have slid away from the end of the wax paper you are holding. Advance your hands along the sides of the paper and grasp the paper just behind the partly rolled roll. Raise paper slowly until the roll rolls forward one more turn. Repeat, but this time the process should be completed and the rolling action should carry the roll into the dish.

Sprinkle the roll with confectioners' sugar. Serve immediately or re-frigerate. Serves 8

Tortoni

1 cup heavy cream
⅓ cup peanut butter
¼ cup sugar
1 teaspoon vanilla

1 egg white
½ cup crushed peanut brittle
½ cup coconut cookie crumbs

Whip the cream until soft peaks form. In a separate mixing bowl, blend the peanut butter, sugar, and vanilla together. Beat the egg white until soft peaks form and fold it into the peanut butter mixture. Combine the peanut brittle and crumbs, and add all but ¼ cup to the peanut butter mixture. Fold in the whipped cream.

Spoon the mixture into 6 paper bake cups or individual dishes or ramekins. Sprinkle with the remaining peanut brittle mix and freeze. Serves 6

Goober Ice Cream

2 egg yolks
½ cup peanut butter
1 teaspoon vanilla

¾ cup brown sugar
Dash of salt
2 cups whipping cream

Beat the egg yolks until light yellow. Add the peanut butter, vanilla, sugar, and salt. Whip the cream and fold it in. Pour the mixture into an ice-cube tray and freeze until frozen 1-inch around the edge. Transfer the ice cream to a chilled bowl, beat until smooth, return to the tray, and freeze until firm. Makes 1 quart

Variation: while the ice cream is in the chilled bowl and after the mixture has been beaten smooth, marbleize with 2 tablespoons of grape jelly or 2 tablespoons of Marshmallow Fluff, and add ½ cup chopped peanuts.

PASTRIES

❧◦◦◦◦◦◦◦◦◦◦◦◦◦◦◦◦◦◦◦◦◦◦◦◦◦☙

Peanut Butter Pie Crust

2 cups sifted all-purpose flour   *½ cup peanut butter*
1 teaspoon salt   *⅓ cup ice water*
⅓ cup shortening

Sift the flour and salt into a mixing bowl. Cut in the shortening and peanut butter with two knives until the mixture has the texture of cornmeal. Add the ice water and stir with a fork to moisten. Refrigerate the pastry for ½ hour, then roll it out on a floured board to ⅛-inch thickness. Line a pie tin with the dough, and prick the bottom and sides with a fork. Bake in a preheated 425° oven for 15 minutes. Makes two 9-inch pie crusts

Peanut Butter Pie Shell

1 cup graham cracker crumbs   *¼ - ⅓ cup peanut butter*

Blend the crumbs and peanut butter together with the fingers and press against the bottom and sides of an 8-inch pie plate. Bake 10 minutes at 375°.

Although the shell can be filled with a variety of fillings, the recipe for Strawberry Cheesecake that follows is especially good.

Strawberry Cheesecake

1 baked Peanut Butter Pie Shell   *2 egg yolks*
(see preceding recipe)   *1 cup sugar*
1 package frozen strawberries   *1 teaspoon vanilla*
2 large packages cream cheese   *¼ cup sour cream*

Defrost the strawberries, drain, and reserve the juice for another purpose. Bring the cream cheese to room temperature and combine with the egg yolks, ⅔ cup of the sugar, and the vanilla. Fill the baked pie shell and bake an additional 20 minutes at 375°. Remove the pie from the oven and allow to cool in the pan.

Cover the cheesecake with strawberries and top with the sour cream mixed with the remaining sugar.

Put in the refrigerator and allow to set for several hours. Serves 6

Banana Chiffon Pie

1 baked Peanut Butter Pie Crust
  (page 80)
1 package of unflavored gelatin
1 cup lukewarm water
2 egg yolks
¼ cup sugar
½ cup peanut butter
½ teaspoon nutmeg

1 teaspoon vanilla
2 egg whites
2 bananas
1 tablespoon lemon juice
½ cup cream, whipped
¼ cup chopped nuts
Candied ginger (optional)

Dissolve the gelatin in ¼ cup of the water. In a saucepan, combine the rest of the water with the egg yolks, 2 tablespoons of the sugar, the peanut butter, and the nutmeg. Cook over low heat until thick, beating constantly with a rotary egg beater (approximately 5 minutes). Stir in the gelatin and vanilla. Chill until slightly thickened.

Beat the egg whites until foamy. Gradually add the remaining sugar and continue to beat until stiff. Fold into the peanut butter mixture.

Slice one banana into the bottom of the baked pie shell. Add the chiffon mixture and chill until stiff. Top with banana slices dipped in lemon juice. Edge with the whipped cream, chopped nuts, and candied ginger. Serves 6

Peanut Cake with Butter Rum Filling

8 eggs, separated
8 tablespoons sugar
5 heaping tablespoons dry bread
   crumbs
5 heaping tablespoons peanut
   butter
FILLING
¼ pound butter

8 tablespoons confectioners'
   sugar
¼ pound ground peanuts
4 tablespoons milk
2 tablespoons light rum
TOPPING
1 cup cream, whipped

Beat the egg yolks and add the sugar gradually, until the mixture is fluffy. Blend in the bread crumbs. Add the peanut butter and beat until well blended. Beat the egg whites until stiff and fold in. Turn into two 8-inch cake pans lined with waxed paper and bake at 300° for 40 to 45 minutes. Remove from the pans immediately and peel off the paper to prevent sticking.

To prepare the filling, cream the butter until fluffy. Beat in the sugar gradually until the mixture is light and fluffy. Combine the peanuts and milk, bring to a boil, cool, and add the rum.

Make a sandwich of the two cake layers with the rum filling in between. Top with the whipped cream.

Peanut Butter Cupcakes

½ cup peanut butter	2 cups sifted all-purpose flour
⅓ cup shortening	2 teaspoons double-acting baking
1 teaspoon vanilla	powder
1½ cups brown sugar	½ teaspoon salt
2 eggs	¾ cup milk

Cream together the peanut butter, shortening, and vanilla. Gradually add the brown sugar, beating until the mixture is light and fluffy. Add the eggs, one at a time, beating well after each.

Sift together the dry ingredients. Add alternately with the milk. Place paper bake cups in muffin pans, and fill half full. Bake in a moderate oven (375°) 20 minutes or until done. Top with peanut butter frosting. Makes approximately 2 dozen cupcakes

Peanut Butter Frosting

4 tablespoons peanut butter	2 tablespoons sifted carob
4 tablespoons honey	powder (see glossary)

Blend the peanut butter, honey, and carob powder together. If the frosting is too thick to spread easily, add water or milk. The frosting will harden. Makes enough for 1 loaf cake

Variation: substitute 4 tablespoons of Marshmallow Fluff for the honey and carob powder.

Peanut Butter–Coconut Frosting

½ cup sugar

3 tablespoons peanut butter

2 cups heavy cream

¾ cup shredded coconut

In the top of a double boiler, gradually stir the cream into the peanut butter and add the sugar. Cook over rapidly boiling water, stirring constantly, until the frosting is thick. Remove from heat, cool, and spread on a baked cake. The recipe makes enough for two 8-inch layers

Apple Sticks

1 egg

1 cup brown sugar

½ cup milk

1 teaspoon vanilla

¼ cup peanut butter

1 cup sifted flour

1 teaspoon double-acting baking powder

1 teaspoon ground cinnamon

Pinch of salt

1 cup peeled and chopped raw   Confectioners' sugar
   apples

If you prefer to blend rather than chop the apples, core them but leave the peel on.

Beat the egg until light and add the sugar gradually, continuing to beat. Add the milk, vanilla, and peanut butter, and blend thoroughly.

Fold in the flour, baking powder, cinnamon, and salt, then the apple.

Spread the mixture in a greased 8-inch square cake pan and bake at 350° for 30 minutes. Cool and cut into slices 1 inch wide and 2 inches long. Roll each slice in confectioners' sugar. Makes approximately 3 dozen sticks

Macaroons

1 egg white   *½ teaspoon vanilla*
¾ cup sugar   *½ cup peanut butter*
½ teaspoon salt

Beat the egg white until it stands in peaks. Add the sugar, salt, and vanilla, then stir in the peanut butter. Use a teaspoon to make rocky heaps, place them on waxed paper on a cookie sheet, and brown in a low oven (275°-300°). Cool and store. Makes 18 to 24 macaroons

© *annabelle pimca*

Crisscross Cookies

1 cup shortening
1 cup granulated sugar
1 cup brown sugar
2 eggs
1 teaspoon vanilla

1 cup peanut butter
3 cups sifted all-purpose flour
2 teaspoons soda
½ teaspoon salt

Cream together the shortening, sugars, eggs, and vanilla. Stir in the peanut butter. Sift the dry ingredients and stir into the creamed mixture. Drop rounded teaspoonfuls on an ungreased cookie sheet. Press each one with the back of a floured fork to make a crisscross. Bake 10 minutes in a 350° oven. Makes approximately 4 dozen cookies

Honey-Orange Cookies

½ cup oil
¾ cup honey
1 egg
½ cup peanut butter
1½ cups whole-wheat flour

1 teaspoon double-acting baking powder
½ teaspoon salt
½-1 cup orange juice
1 teaspoon vanilla

Mix the oil, honey, and egg. Blend in the peanut butter. Combine the flour, baking powder, and salt, and add alternately with the orange juice. Last, add the vanilla. Shape the dough into small balls. Flatten each with a fork. Bake on an ungreased cookie sheet at 350° for 10 minutes. Makes 2 dozen cookies

CANDIES

Peanut Butter Nibbles

1 cup peanut butter
1 cup sifted confectioners'
sugar
2 tablespoons light cream
½ cup finely chopped pecans

½ cup flaked or shredded dried
coconut
⅓ cup graham-cracker crumbs
2 tablespoons butter, melted
2 tablespoons dark molasses

Cream the peanut butter and sugar together. Beat in the cream. Shape the mixture into two rolls, each 1 inch in diameter. Combine the remaining ingredients and pat the mixture around the rolls. Wrap them in wax paper, chill, and cut in ½-inch slices. Makes 2 to 3 dozen candies

Peanut Butter Bars

1 cup peanut butter

⅔ cup softened butter or
   margarine

1 teaspoon vanilla

2 cups firmly packed light-brown
   sugar

3 eggs

1 cup sifted all-purpose flour

½ teaspoon salt

¾ cup sifted 10-X
   (confectioners' powdered)
   sugar

2 teaspoons water

¼ cup semisweet chocolate
   pieces

1 teaspoon shortening

Combine the peanut butter, butter, and vanilla in a large bowl and beat with an electric beater until well blended. Beat in the sugar until the mixture is light and fluffy; then beat in the eggs one at a time.

Stir in the flour and salt, and mix until well blended. Spread the batter in a greased 13x9x2-inch baking pan and bake in a moderate oven (350°) for 35 minutes or until the center springs back when lightly touched with a fingertip. Remove the pan from the oven to a wire rack; cool slightly.

Combine the confectioners' sugar with the water in a small bowl and stir until smooth. Drip from a spoon over the still-warm cookies in the pan. Swirl with the bowl of the spoon to make a random pattern. Melt the chocolate and shortening in the top of a double boiler and drip the mixture over the white glaze. When cool, cut into 36 rectangles. Makes 3 dozen candies

Peanut Butter Crisps

3 cups corn flakes or Product 19
  cereal
1⅓ cups sifted all-purpose flour
½ teaspoon baking soda
½ cup margarine or butter,
  softened
½ cup peanut butter

½ cup granulated sugar
½ cup brown sugar, firmly
  packed
1 teaspoon vanilla
2 eggs
2 tablespoons water

After measuring the cereal, crush it so that it reduces in bulk to 1½ cups. Set aside. Sift together the flour and soda, and set aside.

Place the butter and peanut butter in a large mixing bowl and mix until smooth. Add the sugars and vanilla, and beat until light and fluffy. Separate 1 egg, reserving the white. Add the yolk and 1 whole egg to the peanut butter mixture and beat well. Add the sifted dry ingredients and mix until thoroughly combined. Shape dough into 1-inch balls, using 1 level measuring tablespoon for each ball.

In a small mixing bowl, beat the reserved egg white and the water until foamy. Dip the balls of dough into the egg white mixture, then roll in the crushed cereal. Place the balls on ungreased baking sheets. Flatten each one slightly with the back of a fork or the bottom of a glass. Bake in a moderate oven (350°) about 15 minutes or until lightly browned. Remove immediately from the baking sheets, and cool on wire racks. Makes about 2½ dozen candies

Rum Balls

1 cup peanut butter
1 cup finely grated sweet
  chocolate
1 cup sugar

3 egg whites, lightly beaten
Light rum
½-¾ cup chocolate sprinkles

Mix the peanut butter, chocolate, sugar, and half the egg whites together. Moisten with enough rum to hold the mixture together. Shape into 1-inch balls, roll them in the remaining egg white, and then in the sprinkles. Set them aside to dry.

Keep them for a few days before serving. Makes 30 to 35 balls

American Halvah

½ cup peanut butter
½ cup natural honey

1 teaspoon vanilla
¾-1 cup powdered milk

Blend the ingredients together, gradually adding the powdered milk until the mixture is thick enough to hold its shape. Press to ¾-inch thickness and cut into cubes. Makes 18 to 24 candies

The candy can also be used for stuffing prunes, dates, or figs, or it can be pressed between halves of dried apricots, peaches, or nuts.

Variations: add ½ cup of broken walnuts, small peanuts, chopped blanched almonds, pecans, hazelnuts or Brazil nuts. Or, add ½ to 1 cup of shredded coconut, powdered sugar, or crushed nuts. The mixture can also be made into rolls, which are chilled and cut into slices.

Peanut Butter Fudge

½ cup milk
2 cups sugar
2 tablespoons light corn syrup

1 teaspoon cider vinegar
¼ cup peanut butter
1 teaspoon vanilla

Mix the milk, sugar, syrup, and vinegar together. Cook to a soft-ball stage (234°). Cool to lukewarm. Add the peanut butter and beat until creamy, then add the vanilla. Pour the mixture into a buttered 8-inch square pan and cut into squares.

Variations: before pouring the mixture into the pan, add either 1 cup of marshmallow cream and an additional ½ cup of peanut butter *or* 3 melted squares of unsweetened chocolate and an additional ½ cup of sugar.

- Sesame Chews

1 cup honey
1 cup peanut butter

1 cup carob powder (see
  glossary)

1 cup sesame seeds
1 cup sunflower seeds
½ cup dried shredded coconut

¼ cup dates, or pitted figs, or
  dried apricots, chopped

Heat the honey and peanut butter. Add the rest of the ingredients and mix thoroughly. Pour into an 8-inch square cake pan and refrigerate. Cut into 1-inch squares. Makes 64 candies

Peanut Butter Rounds

½ cup unsalted butter
⅓ cup peanut butter
1 cup fine semolina
1 cup milk

1 cup light cream
½ cup sugar
½ teaspoon vanilla

Melt the butter, add the peanut butter, and cook for 2 minutes over gentle heat. Add the semolina and cook for 30 minutes, stirring constantly.

In a separate pot, bring the milk to a boil, then add the cream and sugar. Simmer until the sugar dissolves, remove from heat, and add the vanilla.

Add the liquid to the cooked semolina, stir and cover, remove from heat, and leave for 15 to 20 minutes.

Roll the mixture into a long sausage, about 1½ inches in diameter, and slice in ½-inch-thick portions. Makes 24 to 36 candies

BEVERAGES

Banana Milkshake

1 small banana
¼ cup peanut butter

1 cup ice cream
1 cup milk

Mash the banana until smooth and place in a blender. Add the peanut butter, the ice cream, and then the milk, and blend until smooth. Makes 2 milkshakes

Peanut Butter Malted Milk

1 tablespoon peanut butter
1 scoop vanilla ice cream
1 tablespoon malt

¼ cup sugar syrup made of equal
parts sugar and water

Blend all the ingredients together and pour into an 8-ounce glass.

Glossary
Mail Order Sources
Index

GLOSSARY OF EXOTIC INGREDIENTS

anise, aniseed   an herb with aromatic seeds, long prized for its many
                  virtues. It was eaten to promote the appetite and still
                  forms the base of many cough medicines. It is most
                  commonly sold ground or in seed form, but can some-
                  times be found dried in the pod (star anise). Keep it
                  in an airtight container.

bean curd   a bland, smooth, custardlike substance made of soy-
                  bean purée that has been pressed into cakes about
                  three inches square and one inch thick. Used as a
                  vegetable, bean curd is high in protein and only needs
                  to be warmed up since it has already been cooked.
                  Extremely versatile (it compliments many Chinese
                  foods), it is sold by the cake, by the pint, and in
                  cans, and is very inexpensive. To store, place in a
                  container, cover with water, and refrigerate. The

bean curd will keep for a week if the water is changed daily.

bean sprouts tiny white shoots with pale green hoods, grown by the Chinese from mung peas. You can grow something comparable by placing beans and peas in an airtight jar, and keeping it in a dark place. After sprouting, the shoots can be kept for another few days if they are covered with water and refrigerated.

bonito flakes dried flakes of the bonito fish, which is related to the mackerel. They are sold in 4-ounce, 8-ounce, and 1-pound boxes in stores specializing in Oriental products.

cardamon an East Indian herb whose seeds are used as a condiment either whole or ground. In India it is used as a digestive employed especially in certain curries and candies.

carob powder ground carob pods, the seeds of the Mediterranean evergreen, which is also called the locust. It is sold in boxes or by the ounce in health-food stores.

cayenne pepper a red, pungent condiment obtained from the fruit or seeds of the *Capsicum* genus, with goat pepper and Guinea pepper being the main sources. It is sold whole or ground and is now readily available in most supermarkets with a good spice rack.

chili pepper   the fruit of *Capsicum frutescens*. Use sparingly if you are not accustomed to the taste. Wash your hands after cutting it, as the juice can be an irritant to the skin or eyes. *See also* cayenne.

chutney   a pungent-tasting combination of fruit seasoned with garlic, chili, mustard, and vinegar, and served as an accompaniment to curry and other Indian dishes. It can be made at home, with apple or mango, or purchased in good supermarkets or specialty shops.

coconut milk   this is made by paring the brown skin from the meat of a fresh ripe coconut, grating the meat, and blending it in an electric blender with 1 cup of fresh scalded milk. Let the milk stand for 20 minutes, then strain. Makes 1½ to 2 cups. One cup of packaged shredded coconut can be used instead of the fresh.

coriander   a European herb of the carrot family, with aromatic fruits *(coriander seeds)* long used as an antiseptic, carminative, and seasoning. It is sold whole or ground, and sometimes the root is also used.

cumin   a dwarf plant native to Egypt and Syria which is

cultivated for its aromatic seeds. It is sold as a ground condiment in most supermarkets, and is an important ingredient in some curry powders.

curry powder   a combination of ground spices including all or at least five of the following: cumin, coriander, cloves, cardamon, cinnamon, mace, bay leaves, black pepper, cayenne, turmeric, mustard seeds. Proportions vary according to the pungency desired. To make a fairly mild and simple curry, start with whole spices and dry-roast, in a 250° oven, 4 ounces each of cloves, black pepper, and cumin; 1 ounce each of cardamon, mace, and cinnamon; and 2 bay leaves. Take care not to burn them. When a rich aroma is given off, remove them from the oven, grind them in a mortar and pass them through a fine sieve or cheesecloth. Store in an airtight jar. The mixture improves with age. You can also make up a curry from spices already ground.

dashi   a fish stock made with seaweed (sold in packages) and bonito flakes (sold in boxes). Place 1 sheet of seaweed and 4 cups of water in a large saucepan and bring to a boil. Lower the flame and allow to simmer for 5 minutes. Remove the seaweed and discard. Take the saucepan off the fire, add ½ cup of bonito flakes and allow the liquid to stand until the flakes sink to the bottom. Strain and use the liquid.

fennel   a perennial European herb of the carrot family culti-
                    vated for its seeds.

ginger   an Asiatic herb with aromatic rootstalks. It is sold
                    green in cans, and *dried,* either in root sections or
                    ground. It is a medicinal stimulant and carminative,
                    as well as a condiment of much versatility. Sections
                    of the root are sometimes *candied.*

lemon balm   a perennial garden herb *(Melissa officinalis)* used as
                    a lemon substitute in salads, chicken and fish dishes,
                    and teas, when it is in season.

pepper oil   oil prepared by frying 1 tablespoon peppercorns
                    (preferably brown Szechwan) in 1 cup peanut oil
                    for 15 minutes. Remove and discard the peppercorns,
                    then pour the pepper oil into a container with a tight-
                    fitting lid and keep for future use.

saffron   the pungent, dried stigmas of a species of crocus
                    flower, used formerly as a dye and now to color and
                    flavor foods. A little goes a long way. It is sold in
                    small quantities.

seaweed   sold dried, in sheets, in small packages in stores
                    specializing in Oriental foodstuffs.

soy oil   oil prepared from soybeans. It is available in health food stores and stores specializing in Oriental food-stuffs.

soy sauce   a Chinese and Japanese sauce made with soybeans that have been subjected to long fermentation, then placed in a brine made of wheat, well water, and sea salt. *See also* tamari.

tamari   a dark soybean sauce which is allowed to age for at least two years before being bottled and sold.

tamarind   a tropical tree of the senna family, whose pod has an acid pulp used for preserves and a cooling laxative drink. It is usually sold compressed into bars. To make *tamarind water,* soak a walnut-sized piece of tamarind in ½ cup of warm water for an hour. Squeeze the tamarind several times in the water, then discard it, and use the liquid.

turmeric   an East Indian herb of the ginger family, used as a yellow dye and medicine, and extensively as a curry ingredient. Because of its medicinal use, it can be purchased in some drugstores, as well as in super-markets.

MAIL ORDER SOURCES

Herbs and Spices

Llama, Toucan and Crow, Inc., 30 Olive St., Greenfield, Mass. 01301

Exotic Ingredients

East

Cardullo's Gourmet Shop, 6 Brattle St., Cambridge, Mass. 02138
George Malko, 185 Atlantic Ave., Brooklyn, N.Y. 11201
Trinacria Importing Co., 415 Third Ave., New York, N.Y. 10016
Tanaka and Co., 326 Amsterdam Ave., New York, N.Y. 10023
Wing Fat Co., 35 Mott St., New York, N.Y. 10013

Midwest

La Preferida, Inc., 177-181 South Water Market, Chicago, Ill. 60608
Kam Shing Co., 2246 Wentworth Ave., Chicago, Ill. 60616

South

Antone's Import Co., 805 Rhode Pl., Houston, Tex. 77001
Oriental Import-Export Co., 2009 Polk St., Houston, Tex. 77001

West

Haig's, 441 Clement St., San Francisco, Calif. 94118

Canada

Main Importing Co., 1188 St. Lawrence, Montreal 126, Quebec
Sayfy's Groceteria, 265 Jean Talcon East, Montreal 327, Quebec

INDEX